Pencil transfer drawing and (opposite) engraving
of the greater spotted woodpecker

THOMAS BEWICK'S
BIRDS

WATERCOLOURS AND

ENGRAVINGS

❊❊❊

The MIT Press

CAMBRIDGE, MASSACHUSETTS

First MIT Press edition, 1982
First published in 1981 by
The Gordon Fraser Gallery Ltd, London and Bedford
Copyright © Gordon Fraser Gallery 1981

Library of Congress catalog card number: 81-84994

ISBN 0-262-02176-5

Printed at The Roundwood Press, Kineton, Warwick
Designed by Peter Guy

LIST OF PLATES

❖

A NOTE ON BEWICK

Thomas Bewick (1753-1828) is known to the world for his marvellous wood-engravings of birds, animals and country scenes. Even those to whom his name means nothing are likely to have seen his work used to decorate tins, boxes and wrappings, for his appeal is universal.

As a boy, his gifts were already apparent. He would draw compulsively, on the floor, on the hearth, on his thumbnail, even on gravestones. Around the time of his fourteenth birthday, after a schooling punctuated by truancy and floggings, Bewick was apprenticed to Ralph Beilby, a general engraver. Most of his work was in metal, often inscribing coats of arms or mottoes for learned and wealthy customers. Although there was no real training in draughtsmanship, Bewick's natural talent flowered, and he began to engrave from his own designs. His illustrations for a series of fables for children won him a prize awarded by the Society for the Encouragement of Arts Manufactures and Commerce. Such was the measure of his skill that only a year after the completion of his apprenticeship he was in partnership with his former employer. From this moment, he never looked back.

Thomas Bewick is perhaps best remembered for the two-volume *History of British Birds* (1797-1804). It combined his love of nature with his great attention to detail, and the result was far superior to anything seen before. Wherever possible, Bewick drew from life. When he could not find a live specimen, he had to rely on stuffed birds in museums, but took immense care to be as true to life as his researches could allow.

Bewick would start by producing a detailed water-colour drawing. From this he would make an outline sketch to the required size. The back of this transfer drawing would then be rubbed with a soft lead pencil. Placing the drawing on the block, and folding down the overlap, Bewick would then score around the outlines with a fine point. The outline of the image thus transferred to the block, Bewick would engrave carefully, using the original, detailed drawing as his reference. A transfer drawing and the engraving made from it are reproduced as the frontispiece and on the title page.

At the time, illustration was normally in the form of crude woodcuts. From his training as an engraver, Bewick learned how to work on the hard end-grain of boxwood in order to achieve accurate and detailed results. His combination of flair and precision was passed on to a generation of apprentices, and the great success of his books led to many imitations of both his style and his method. In the welter of praise which has attended his engraving over the years, the marvellous watercolour drawings (of which around 400 exist) have remained virtually unnoticed. The selection in this book has been drawn from Iain Bain's masterly *The Watercolours and Drawings of Thomas Bewick and his Workshop Apprentices,* which presents them for the first time in a major study. The publishers are grateful to Iain Bain, Sir Geoffrey Keynes, the Trustees of the British Museum and the National History Society of Northumbria for permission to reproduce works in their possession.

All the illustrations in this book are by Thomas Bewick except for those on pp. 8, 27 and 28 which were engraved from his drawings by apprentices, and (ironically) the bird named after him, Bewick's swan (p. 16), which is by his son Robert; all are reproduced in their original sizes.

THE ROBIN

A tame garden bird in Britain, a shy woodland bird elsewhere, the robin was chosen as Britain's national bird in 1961, although it had been the object of national affection for centuries.

The robin puts its scarlet breast and its pleasant warbling song to good use in fiercely defending its territory against intruding birds of its own kind. [Length 5½ inches]

THE CHAFFINCH

The chaffinch is one of the most widespread and common of birds, breeding wherever there are trees and bushes. It is also one of the most attractive birds, showing a fine variety of colours.

It has a fine bustling, cheerful song, which is remarkable for its regional differences. Even within Britain local dialects can be detected, although its alarm call of 'pink-pink' is universal. [Length 6 inches]

THE SPARROWHAWK

The sparrowhawk, a secretive bird of wooded country, is a great predator of small birds, which it pursues with great agility. Its method is one of surprise attack, whether dashing out of its tree after a passing bird, or hedge-hopping in open country, flying low along one side of a hedgerow, and then darting up and over to pluck a small unsuspecting bird feeding on the other side.

The sparrowhawk is happily recovering its numbers after persecution by game-keepers and suffering from the effect of toxic chemicals. [Length: male 11 inches, female 15 inches]

THE PIED FLYCATCHER

The pied flycatcher is primarily a bird of deciduous woodland, although it has colonised other areas where there are nesting holes. The provision of nest boxes in some areas has been of significant help.

The bird only partially lives up to its name, in that only the breeding male is truly pied. The female, and male outside the breeding season, are olive-brown. The bird does not feed exclusively on insects caught on the wing, but also takes insects and caterpillars from the tree foliage. [Length 5 inches]

THE CROSSBILL

The crossbill is an attractive finch, and is almost always associated with conifers. The adult male is generally brick-red, while the female is olive-green. Its most remarkable feature is its bill, the tips of which are crossed so that it can extract seeds from fir cones, which provide its almost exclusive diet.

The cone crop fluctuates, and as a result the crossbill periodically erupts from its breeding areas in search of new feeding grounds. [Length 6½ inches]

THE GREEN WOODPECKER

The green woodpecker is found in all types of wood-ed country, where it may be located by its un-mistakable bright yellow rump, best seen when the bird is making its slow, undulating flight, or by its ringing call or 'yaffle'.

It has a liking for ants, which means that it spends more time than other woodpeckers on the ground, probing with its long bill, and then scooping up the ants with its tongue. [Length 12½ inches]

THE REDSTART

The male redstart outshines the duller female, although both birds share the vivid russet tail from which the bird gets its name. 'Steort' is an Old English word for 'tail'.

As with many other species, distinctive plumage plays a major part in the bird's courtship display. The male chooses a female and courts her by splaying his tail feathers to show a blaze of red.

The redstart will breed in any habitat where holes can be found for nesting. [Length $5\frac{1}{2}$ inches]

THE BRENT GOOSE

The Brent goose is a small, dark-headed goose, heavily dependent on its winter diet of eelgrass. When the grass temporarily disappeared in the 1930s, the geese became very scarce.

The Brent goose is very much a sea bird, only coming to land to breed. It both rests and roosts on the sea. [Length 22-24 inches]

THE AMERICAN REDSTART

The American Redstart is a strikingly attractive North American wood warbler which has only been recorded twice in the British Isles. [Length 5-5½ inches]

[9]

THE DEMOISELLE CRANE

A beautiful marsh bird with a conspicuous white
ear-tuft. [Length 38 inches]

THE BLACKCAP

The blackcap gets its name from the male's sooty black cap (the female has a rust-coloured cap). It is famous for its melodious song, a sweet, powerful and rather jerky warble, which has earned it the mis-nomer of 'the northern nightingale'. It nests in thick undergrowth in woods, heaths and gardens.

  Like other warblers, blackcaps feed mainly on insects, although before migration they change to a fruit diet to fuel them for their journey. Some black-caps, in fact, are stained purple at this time from the elderberries and blackberries of their new diet. [Length 5½ inches]

THE WILLOW WARBLER

The Willow warbler is a small leaf warbler with olive-brown upper parts and yellowish-white underparts.

It is almost impossible to identify by sight alone because of its likeness to another leaf warbler, the chiff-chaff. The two birds can be distinguished only by their calls. The chiff-chaff's song, a monotonous 'chiff-chaff' contrasts with the willow warbler's song, a fluent, mellow series of descending notes.

The two birds were first distinguished by the eighteenth-century naturalist Gilbert White.
[Length $4\frac{1}{4}$ inches]

THE MARSH TIT

A small, neat, black-capped bird, the marsh tit poses severe problems of identification for the bird-watcher because of its similarity to another tit, the willow tit.

The two birds can only be safely identified by their differing songs, and by their nesting habits: the willow tit excavates its own nest, whereas the marsh tit employs natural holes.

The marsh tit is not in fact a marshland bird, and the willow tit has no preference for willows: both are woodland birds. [Length 4½ inches]

THE GREENFINCH

The greenfinch is unmistakable with its strongly
coloured plumage, chunky body and long wings.

It is a very familiar bird, hardly ever found away
from human settlements. In particular, it is a
common visitor to suburban bird tables, where it
exploits the delights of sunflower seeds and peanuts.

In the breeding season, the male defends his territory with a long-drawn, nasal 'dzhwee' note.
[Length 5 inches]

THE GREAT CRESTED GREBE

These handsome birds were almost exterminated in
Britain in the nineteenth century, for their feathers
were used to adorn women's hats. But now, with a
change in fashion and the spread of reservoirs and
gravel pits, they have happily more than recovered
their numbers. [Length 19 inches]

BEWICK'S SWAN

A truly wild bird, this visitor from the Arctic has a
yellow face which is so variable that individual
birds can be identified. The swan is named in honour
of Thomas Bewick. [Length 48 inches]

THE TREE SPARROW

The tree sparrow is a rather nondescript brown
seed-eating bird, only slightly more attractive than
the familiar house sparrow, the tree sparrow's
bright chestnut crown and slimmer, cleaner build
giving it a slight edge over its urban cousin.

In Europe, it is mainly to be found in wooded
areas, near fields or farmland for feeding. It nests in
holes in the trees, in colonies or scattered groups.
Colonies may build up rapidly, and then equally
quickly disappear. As yet, there is no explanation for
this which is perhaps the bird's most interesting
and unusual characteristic. [Length 5½ inches]

THE HAWFINCH

The hawfinch is a bird of mature woodland and orchard. Despite being Britain's largest finch, with an outsize bill and striking wing bars, it is a shy bird and notoriously difficult to see, particularly when feeding in the treetops.

Its enormous bill is used to crack nuts, kernels and fruit stones. It has been estimated as being capable of exerting pressures of over 150 pounds per square inch, more than sufficient to crack open cherry stones or crush hornbeam seeds, its favourite foods. [Length 7 inches]

THE TREECREEPER

The treecreeper is a small brown-and-white bird with a long curved beak, and is found in woodland of all types.

It is well camouflaged and very difficult to see as it forages for insects on the trunks and branches of trees. When noticed, it bears a remarkable resemblance to a mouse as it works its way in a series of spasmodic jerks up the trunk of a tree before fluttering down to start again at the base of the next tree.

In severe weather, the treecreeper protects itself by roosting in a sheltered crevice behind the bark. [Length 5 inches]

THE WHITETHROAT

The whitethroat is the least secretive of warblers, and an occupant of hedge and scrub of all kinds.

In the breeding season, the male is particularly conspicuous in its vertical, chattering song-flight from which it plunges back into cover, and also when singing its 'wichity-wichity' song while perched on a bush.

The whitethroat also possesses a rather violent courtship display, in which the male follows the female as if to attack her. The female responds by darting at the male, whereupon at the last moment he turns aside. [Length $5\frac{1}{2}$ inches]

THE LAMMERGEIER

OR BEARDED VULTURE

This large vulture has a strange habit of dropping
bones from a height to extract the marrow. [Length
40-45 inches]

THE GREAT AUK

A flightless bird, exploited for its meat, eggs and
skin, this luckless creature was finally exterminated
in 1844. [Length 30 inches]

THE REDWING

The redwing is the smallest thrush to be found in Britain, and is mainly a winter visitor from Northern Europe. It is distinguished by its prominent white eye stripe, and red patches on flanks and under wing.

Redwings roost communally at night, and at dusk can be seen diving into bushes, usually rhododendron or hawthorn. They suffer particularly badly from severe winters, when the earth is too frozen for them to dig up their food. At such times they will enter town centres in search of food. [Length $8\frac{1}{4}$ inches]

THE NUTCRACKER

The nutcracker is a rare winter visitor to Britain, mainly from Siberia and southern Scandinavia. It is a bird of coniferous forest, and has a long bill, a brown body spotted with white, black wings and a black and white tail. It feeds principally on conifer seeds but also likes hazelnuts, which it cracks open with its sharp bill. The nutcracker has a unique habit of storing pine seeds to feed its young in specially adapted pouches in the floor of its mouth. [Length 12½ inches]

THE RED-NECKED PHALAROPE

The red-necked phalarope only shows its red (or, more accurately, bright orange) neck in summer. It is a small wader which swims rather than wades and spends most of the time out at sea, although it can be very tame when it does come to land.

The bird has a curious feeding technique which involves spinning like a top in order to bring food to the surface of the water. [Length 7 inches]

THE NIGHT HERON

The night heron, characteristically hunched up when at rest, nocturnal and skulking in its habits, a bird not easily seen. Though it is a rare visitor to Britain, escaped birds have established a wild colony in Edinburgh Zoo. [Length 24 inches]

THE RED-BREASTED MERGANSER

The red-breasted merganser is a diving duck with a narrow saw-edged bill, so designed to enable it to hang on to its slippery prey of fish.

It is an accomplished diver, sometimes staying under water for as long as two minutes, when it will use its wings as well as its feet to chase its prey. It will also fish by swimming with only its head submerged.

Only the male bird possesses a red breast. [Length 23 inches]

THE TUFTED DUCK

A success story, the tufted duck was unknown as a breeding duck in Britain until the mid-nineteenth century, yet today it is one of the most successful. It has skilfully exploited new man-made habitats such as reservoirs and gravel pits to extend its breeding range. Its tolerance of man allows it to breed successfully even on park lakes in towns, where it can become very tame, supplementing its natural diet with handouts of bread. [Length 17 inches]

THE LITTLE GREBE

Grebes are aquatic birds with lobed toes, and the smallest of the family is the little grebe, normally known as the dabchick.

Although more shy in its habits than other grebes, its presence often only betrayed by its strange high-pitched whinnying call, it is quite widespread, and can be found even on town ponds or lakes. [Length 6 inches]

THE NIGHTINGALE

The nightingale is a plump, rufous-brown thrush, best known for the beauty, power and variety of its song which, as its name suggests, it also delivers at night.

  The bird is skulking and secretive in its habits, and despite its explosive calls, is very difficult to see in its woodland home. [Length 6½ inches]

THE CURLEW

The curlew is a large grey-brown wader with long
legs and a large, downward-curving bill. The bill,
used to best effect when probing for small animals
in the mud, may be as long as 5 inches.

  Curlews, however, are rightly famous for their
call, which is often the first sign of the bird's presence. It is an eery, melancholic 'coor-lee' which
blends beautifully with the wild and lonely moorland, bog and estuary which the bird inhabits.
[Length 22 inches]

THE BLACK GUILLEMOT

The black guillemot is a black-and-white seabird
with distinctive red feet. A member of the auk
family, it is smaller and less gregarious than its
relation, the guillemot, preferring to breed in pairs
or groups rather than noisy colonies. Parties of
these birds can be seen swimming together, when
they adopt a regimental attitude, forming ranks or
lines.

 The black guillemot is also less likely to be seen far
out to sea, preferring to stay sheltered within a
reasonable distance of land. [Length 13½ inches]

THE JACKDAW

The jackdaw is an intelligent bird, full of character.
It engages in acrobatic flying displays; its curiosity
causes it to steal a variety of bright objects, and it
can even be taught to 'talk'.

A successful bird, it lives in a variety of habitats
from sea cliff to town centre, and eats virtually anything. [Length 13 inches]

THE CUCKOO

The cuckoo evokes mixed feelings; the male's courtship call, by which the bird gets its name, is a symbol
of spring in Britain, whereas its parasitic breeding
habits seem quite repugnant.

The female will lay her own egg in the occupied
nest of a small bird, disposing of one of the host
bird's eggs by way of deception. The young cuckoo,
on hatching, will eject all the remaining eggs of the
host bird in order to ensure the undivided attention
of its unfortunate foster parents. [Length 13 inches]

THE RUFF

In summer, the male developes a huge ruff around its neck and ear tufts. This ruff varies in colour between individual birds, and may be shades of purple-brown, black, chestnut, yellow or white.

Ruffs congregate ahead of the reeves (the females) at their traditional communal display grounds or 'leks', where they engage in mock combat to assert their right to mating territories. When the reeves arrive each will select her mate by preening his ruff. Not surprisingly, the males with the most resplendent ruffs are the most successful in attracting a mate. [Length: male 11 inches, female 19 inches]

THE DUNLIN

The dunlin has a thin, slightly down-curved beak, which it uses to probe for small molluscs and other animals in tidal mudflats and along the shore line.

It is often regarded as the typical small shore bird, yet flying in dense packs, performing aerobatics in perfect unison, the dunlin presents an amazing spectacle. It has been known by a bewildering variety of names: ox-bird, plover-splage, sea-snipe and stint, and can be remarkably tame.

The dunlin is a common, stout-bodied wader, with a rufous-brown back and black belly in summer; in winter its back is grey-brown and its belly grey-white. [Length 7 inches]

THE TAWNY OWL

The tawny owl, a bird of deciduous woodland, parks and large gardens or indeed any area with scattered trees, is for many people the archetypal owl.

It hunts by night, but its presence during the day, roosting hunched up in a tree, is often given away by the clamour of small birds mobbing the predator. [Length 15 inches]

THE MEADOW PIPIT

Although quite profuse in moorland and almost any kind of open country, the meadow pipit is a favourite prey of the merlin, and the cuckoo's number one choice as host bird to its parasitic young.

It is most easily distinguished from the otherwise similar tree pipit by its call: as opposed to that bird's 'teez', the meadow pipit seems to utter a sharp feet-feet-feet'. This could be taken as a reminder of another difference: the tree pipit has a highly curved hind claw to provide purchase on a branch, whereas the meadow pipit, a ground bird, has a long, straight rear claw. [Length 5¾ inches]

THE YELLOWHAMMER

The yellowhammer is a bird of farmland and open country, and as with most other buntings, seed-eating birds with short, thick-set beaks, the male is a very handsome bird indeed, with bright yellow and chestnut plumage.

The yellowhammer's monotonous but pleasant song, often written as 'little bit of bread and no cheese' and rendered from an exposed perch, typifies for many people a languid day spent in the countryside in summer. [Length 6½ inches]

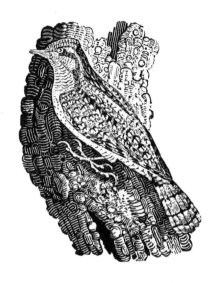

THE WRYNECK

The wryneck is an ant-eating woodpecker which gets its name from its unusual courtship display, as it twists its head right round on its neck. [Length 6½ inches]

THE BULLFINCH

Another bird which evokes mixed feelings: the bullfinch is admired for its handsome plumage; the black-capped, pink-breasted male is particularly resplendent. It is, however, hated for the damage it does to fruit trees and ornamental shrubs. A very methodical feeder, it carefully strips trees by working its way to the end of each branch. It has been known to strip up to 30 buds per minute.

Bullfinches generally travel in pairs, and although evidence is difficult to find, it is believed that they mate for life. [Length 5¾ inches]

THE GOLDFINCH

One of the most pleasant among sights and sounds is a 'charm' of goldfinches alighting on a patch of thistles. These small finches are beautiful in appearance, delightful to hear, and amusing to watch. The adults are an elegant mixture of red, gold and black; their call, a liquid 'tswitt-witt-witt', has a unique tinkling quality, and they are acrobatic feeders.

Unfortunately, although protected in Britain, they are still caught to be caged as pets in some other countries. [Length 4¾ inches]

THE WREN

The wren is a tiny red-brown bird easily recognised by its characteristic perky stance with cocked-up tail, and by its remarkably loud and piercing song.

An adaptable bird, it has colonised a wide variety of habitat. The wren is found in towns, on hilltops, in forests, on sea-cliffs and even on rocky oceanic islands.

Wrens also possess amazing powers of recovery. They feed principally on insects and spiders, and therefore many die from starvation in severe winters, as they cannot be assisted by artificial feeding. However, within a few years, they invariably regain their former numbers. [Length $3\frac{3}{4}$ inches]

THE WHINCHAT

The whinchat is a slim, elegant bird with striped dark upperparts, a noticeable white eye-stripe and rufous-orange underparts extending to its chin.

  It prefers heath or rough grassland with bracken and low bushes, and it feeds on butterflies, moths, and flies taken mainly from grass stalks.

  It is a migratory bird, never wintering in western Europe. It arrives in Britain for the summer after a journey across the Sahara from tropical Africa. [Length 5 inches]

THE BLUE TIT

Originally a woodland bird, the blue tit now exploits the garden bird table, where its acrobatic feeding habits make it a firm favourite. It has learnt to solve a number of feeding problems, including how to prise off milk bottle tops. [Length $4\frac{1}{2}$ inches]

The Bunting

61

THE CORN BUNTING

Though it bears a rather dull brown plumage, this
largest of buntings is a surprisingly enigmatic bird.
Its distribution seems almost arbitrary, in that some
appropriate open country contains none, until one
crosses an imaginary corn bunting 'border' to find
them proliferating. The bird shares another curious
form of behaviour with humans in that whereas
some males are strictly monogomous, others will
mate with a number of females. The corn bunting's
song sounds remarkably like the jangling of a bunch
of keys. It flies, surprisingly, with its legs hanging
limply down. [Length 7 inches]

THE DOTTEREL

The dotterel is a most distinctive plover in its summer plumage, with its white eye stripes, chestnut underparts and black belly. The dotterel nests on the ground at high altitude, when it can be remarkably tame. It is also unusual in that the female is the dominant partner. Slightly larger and more attractive than the male, she takes the initiative in courtship display. After she has laid her eggs, she allows the male to incubate them and rear the chicks, often leaving him in order to find another mate. [Length 8½ inches]

THE WIGEON

The gregarious wigeon is to be found by rivers and marshland in wooded country. The drake has an unmistakable whistling call, 'wheeyoo', which is very penetrating, and is easily recognised by the many wildfowlers who hunt this bird. The duck's response is an oddly purring or low growling sound.

The drake has a chestnut and cream head, pink breast and grey back. Its high forehead and stubby bill give it a rather huddled appearance. The wigeon is a vegetarian, and grazes on marsh and moor, sometimes in concert with the Brent goose, which shares its liking for eelgrass. [Length 18 inches]

THE SKYLARK

The skylark, a bird of open ground, is justly famous for the quality and variety of its warbling song.

The song is delivered as the bird ascends vertically to a great height, and is continued as the skylark hovers and then plunges back to earth. The song-flight can last as long as five minutes.

Unfortunately, the bird is taken in considerable numbers, as in some countries it is regarded as a great table delicacy. [Length 7 inches]

THE BLACKBIRD

Another bird which has increased its range and numbers by exploiting man-made habitats, the blackbird is now probably the most common resident breeding in Britain. It has a beautiful song, mellow and fluting, which is mainly to be heard at dawn and dusk. [Length 10 inches]

THE GREAT BUSTARD

An attempt is now being made to re-introduce the great bustard to Britain as a breeding species after a hundred and fifty years' absence. [Length: male 40 inches, female 30 inches]

THE SHORT-EARED OWL

The short-eared owl hunts in open country by day as well as at dusk, principally seeking out voles and mice. It is nomadic, and will congregate in any area where there is a temporary surplus of its prey.

The 'ears' by which the bird gets its name have no hearing function: they are, in fact, small tufts of feathers. [Length 14½ inches]